Enough Said

By

Ferris E. Jones

ISBN: 978-81-19654-47-5

First Edition: 2024
Rs. 200/-

Cybarwit.net
HIG 45 Kaushambi Kunj, Kalindipuram
Allahabad - 211011 (U.P.) India
http://www.cyberwit.net
Tel: +(91) 9415091004
E-mail: info@cyberwit.net

Printed at Repro India Limited.

This book is dedicated to

Ed Jones

“Enough said”

Contents

Morsel

1
Shopping
without cash
Is an
eighteen-year-old girl
missing her period.

2
Spend your time listening
and others will
dream of you more.

3
Body art
means far less
to God
then abortions.

4
Getting rid
of social security
will be in conflict
with religion.

5
He's a
mule skinner
you sweet
little tomato.

6
An actor is
what mankind
strives to become.

7
Women know
their child's soul,
yet never finds
out why
their men lie.

8
Television twists the outcome faster
than plain folk
can see a child fall.

9
Retail kills,
mames, names,
and cries like
a bitch,
all the way
to the bank.

10
My dog died,
and my
wife cried.

11
You sit
and fucking
listen,
I'm going to
get my gun.

12
I was in
the L.A earthquake,
and my U2 tape
skipped.

13
Why buy
a book
to change
your life.
Don't you already
know how?

14
All faculties focus
finally on a thought,
that stops sleep.
Maybe now,
knowing
the years,
the learning
can begin.

15
That pillow thing,
looks like
you have and
anal ring
around your neck.

16
He's a fine man,
but what's up
with his kids?

17
Speak to king
Richard yourself,
or shut up.

18
Barbecue this !!

19
Speak, shit,
sit, or fart,
the beer
is still cold.

20
Fans
only blow
your own
smell
in your
face.

21
Sit, have
a cookie,
feel like
you should have
brought a gift.

22
She's not
your mother.
She's the lesbian
sister of
your other
brother Darrel.

23
The bottle
of mercury
holds the
old man's
future.

24
The balance
of power
rests in
an upside down
black can.

25
The car
spoke sideways.
Well, he
is sixteen.

26
There
once
was
a
keg.

27
A Murder
victim can
come back
to stay.

28
What year
is this?
Detox
is a bitch.

29
The mirror has
my stuff.
My wife
has my soul.

30
A house
will fall
to Satan,
when the
drink pours
and the sun
goes down.

31
Mike makes
Micky Mouse
run, run, run
to grandma's
house.

32
A stone house
in the mountains
is where my
childhood is buried.

33
Stealing
from friends
is the
murdering
of a soul.

34
A silent
death
means a
silent
existence.

35
I am gold.
You may
move over
now, fucker.

36
We see
only
what we
want, not
what the
ghosts
want us
to see.

37
A bus to
San Fran,
a Van Halen
groupie,
that's
a trip.

38
Well,
I better go,
we are
going to get
stoned now.

39
If I had
a brother,
and he
was alive,
our fights,
would be
formidable.

40
Miserable
by his
own hands,
time is
running out.

41
I have come,
see my face,
I am
the sun.

42
There is
only one
I can see.

43
A tormented
Soul has
the eyes,
of a
dying dog.

44
I've been
There,
seen it.
Believe it,
it's real.

45
The city
in the sea
hides the
secrets of
what to be.

46
Men are
not
meant
to have
chains.

47
Mushroom me
Shroomie.

48
It comes
without
you.

49
A X,
tear drops.
a question mark,
a star.

Ritalin

I'm miserable,
I ignored your name,
little brother.
A teeming,
roaring pace.
I wondered often.
I could capture myself,
not awful, just neglected.
No remedy,
solely age
A guarantee of growing
your predecessor,
hovers.
I took care of those waltzes
and stood confounded at your route.
I still receive,
troubles mine.
As of today,
ratified in time.

Freedom

Leaves into slumber,
swirled by each day,
the sunlight's plunder.

Pleasant thoughts
appear to wander.
The night's message
does not squander.

Freedom begs
from a love lost hard.
The answer is here,
it rests in the yard.

Dungeon

I beseech you
lingering moments,
stop.
Your insect has its eggs
in my thoughts.
Open this dungeon.
Set the criminal free.
This sentence is relentless.

Let me roam the night,
have the pictures
in color.
Remember fondly
the boy,
the frogs diving
from the sky.
They were alive.

A Smile Inside

I never wish
for a slimmer walk.
Take from the sky,
to hear you talk.

Its tender cottage
of renewals crown.
The smiles laugh
at Satan's frown.

I have you uncaged,
with ample stride.
The gaze of emotion,
with a smile inside.

Nest

He tossed
his intentions
from the nest.
If they take off,
they continue.
If they don't,
they perish.

The gulag
rests on
the stoop,
like a
southern
hound dog
in the
hot sun.

Death Song

(From the Palm of God)

Anointed will be his grip,
scoured of the sinner's blood.
Grey mane will flow and
death, you will know.

When the eyes of fire you mourn,
lie restive and worn.
Weep not for the throne,
its scale does not speak,
of reasons or what you seek.

Serve this day, its thunder neat.
By his side, you'll take your seat.

> "I am He who lives, and was dead,
> And behold, I am alive forevermore.
> Amen. And I have the keys of Hades
> And of death".

Awful

The mitt rocks
with the movement
of the tools.
Sunny homes change.
I'll be there rapidly.
I study another
as he goes.
His childlike face mangled.
Creation has abandoned him.
    What are you looking at?
    you ugly little fucker?
    You're ugly, you know that?
The sky turned mysterious.
The lights are off,
No one is home.
    He could hear within me.
    He is right.
    I am the ugly one.

Fury

Fleeing and twisting the
reptile sings,
"Fury is not mine,
fury is thine".

The prophet brings God milk,
The snared brings the wine.
"Fury is not mine,
fury is thine".

With no lips to whisper,
the scornful rest,
a cornerstone in their crypt.
"Fury is not mine,
fury is thine".

Land of Wine

My wine, mixed with water
witnesses the redeemed
and righteous.

In new moons, troubles come.
Yet, I shall not be in fear of a purge
in this land of idols.

The path is full of treasure.
Shake the ground and silver falls
from the teeth of moles.

A mighty man will judge
the oppressor's stand.
Plunder will be as wine
that plights their land.

Commencement Speech

For a long time
I embraced being different.
Then, the phone rings
and the glory of the sunset
disappears. Gone,
changed forever
I weep.
Who will stand with me?

Society has chosen
to reward those who
criticize others.
Where is my place?
Do I stay and fight?
Live in fear?
Stay silent?
Wait until the glory
begs for a return.
Will it come with birth
or death?

Selfish Time

Selfish time
muddles minds,
twisting, beseeching,
clanging gates
not meant to be sealed.
I see you, not as usual.
Your picture floats
between the bars,
with hostile nights,
inaccessible stars.

Hidden

Slowly, he will take,
never pondering
a conclusion.
He loiters in your walk,
begs in your talk,
breeds in seclusion.

Created with symmetry,
Proportion never wavers
on this mission.
He is never careless,
never restless,
holds no ambition.

America

Yeah,
I cut down
the cherry tree,
wrecked the car,
shot Old Yeller.
Then, I took
the kids
for ice cream.
It is real,
the dream,
see it?

A New Start

Darker thoughts, dimmed, dead
in this perfect month. Ghosts
dance to a friendly tune. Pivotal
the future starts today.

A man, released by his name
fends for himself. With emotion,
he glows honestly, unopposed.
Sea eyes, he rests on the quay.

Our Fasting

The fasting ends today,
rings have been exchanged,
wine shall be shared.

No affliction to bring down,
no fury, no sound.
My Sabbath remains.

Our fists wave at the dishonest,
uncovering an angel's peace.

Blowing waters flow,
unprotecting the corporate beast.

Tuesday Night

Walking, I cried,
by the light.

The moon said,
"perception is everything,
the reality was squandered,
by you, in youth".

Sunflower

Twilight's grasp
of light's
spinning whispers,
race the syllables of imagination.
Time will bend,
this realm will weaken,
painting my heart,
the color of Eden.

I'm not Coming

Desert hole,
wrought iron, rusted,
adorned patterns,
old ground.

An embrace,
stretching,
carpeting,
the care is in,
this resting place.

Tall, thin, old,
see history,
brag of war,
their stories.

Leaves swing,
days contemplate,
capture tranquility's
connection to death.

Remember Today

Time is an echo,
a glimpse
of what was.
Old tales sit,
in souls untold.

We danced with Dionysus
and floated the early sea.
Died a thousand times,
both you and me.

Toss out all your fears,
and our souls will remember.
It's all in the past,
those long-heard tears.

Every Hour on the Hour

Weaving pain as a companion,
sorrow dwells in your shadow.
Wounds unseen to grieve,
deep as a seed canyon.

The lingering weight latches,
a mistake takes power.
Scars fight for freedom,
every hour on the hour.

Our Last Dance

The passage of themes
is a mingling dance.
The map prevails,
over her silver resilience.

Her laughter's wisdom
strums every wrinkle.
The fears, the stars,
God did sprinkle.

A story will be spoken
of a crown's rare eye.
Her love will wait
until she ascends up high.

Judging Eyes

Judging eyes
cast a shadow
on the fool.

Laughter taunts
the cruel day.
Scorn is truth,
Wisdom lies.
Mocking bliss
Kills their eyes.

As they jest,
A fool they see
I stand with armor
Grace for you
And grace for me.

Old Jesus

Old, bearded gray he walks.
Thorns of ancient grace
still etched, still guide
his eyes.

He approaches
The gaze upon the sorrow
As he is sacrificed
In the pain of others.

An offering is witnessed,
yet, no man speaks.
A testament is written,
And no man shrieks.

Behind this rock, I
stand besides,
waiting for the cloud
they say he rides.

A Boy's First Crush

The symphony of its symmetry
plays upon the sun's vision.
The pitch of jubilation
Brings hope home.

The children's chatter steals
young minds.
Revealing, in this playground,
All that binds.

The Green Tint of Her Summer Hair

The green tint
of the summer hair
smiles laughter.
The 1974 colors dance,
a T-shirt soars.

Blond trails stream
the hillside.
Time discusses itself
as it unfolds
the weight - bearing grass
of her shadow.

Together again
in every thread,
the moon begins
its day. The
telling of your life,
with its vast complaint,
and sudden end.

Reservoir

My son, his son,
pass the bonds of wisdom.
Unravel with patience.
The legacy
gets devoured today.

The beacon, the Deacon
shines in the moment,
when deep fish
get enshrined
in years.

Search this treasure
and conceal its map.
in this day's bliss,
that the aged
has found his wish.

Old and Getting Older

The mower smokes,
crooked lines
become hours.

Paths will cross,
revealing the day
Witnessed by trees.
the imperfect way

Free with hope
Each twist plays a part.
Rest in the curves,
as this journey
does in your heart.

The Earth Spins

Low, in the branches
of the forest,
resides a rare creature.

His confines hide his color,
his sunlight is endless
as he cloths the forest's deck.

He comes to speak with rain,
prefers the dawns gaze,
while the birds fear his ways.

Unaware of his slither,
the blue worm talks,
as a lonely human walks.

Two Worlds

Cute, a restaurant smirk,
sits us far away
from the door.
I imagine the somber,
sullen, black and white
countertops of summer.
Hot, the history
can be tasted.
The courage stands
with the sound
of cutlery,
and hate.
We drink in
the music, the laughter.
Two worlds, decades apart
hold society. I sit
in their place,
understanding my chair
is not the same
as their stool. I have
no stories, no battles.
We received a conversation,
and they were received -
as an agitation.

Time

Celestial,
the beings are free.
They soar
without air, on the
gravity currents
of the planets.
Light flashes,
light bends,
light disappears.

The hum
of a vacuum,
cannot travel,
but it's there.
Melodies are played
on the rings
of galaxies. Life,
weightless, and
in wonder.

Dust travels,
searching for
a blessed
playground.
Where time
is made,
created
by human
hands.

Solitude

Turmoil, rush, and roar,
the quiet of life dies.
No tranquil space for
secrets to hide.
I ask for nothing,
time, be on my side.

No judgements to craft,
for wandering space.
It's the gem in time
that soars in desire
collecting one's fate.

There's depth is sound,
pounding the stillness dead.
Unburdened silence leaks
Into a stillness,
perfect for my head.

The Right and Left Hand of God

Fighting for your life
brings with it
a good death.
How many baby daddies
That bitch have,
anyway?

Food and love
provided, paves
for the future.
When was the last time
she held a job,
not just you?

The right words are simple,
the wrong words can
bring tag along death.
When did she love
you last,
or cast,
your eye?

Death of an Angel

Above, the dance
of gold and bright
rests cold, mournful.

The spirt, mortal,
wounded, the story
plays for all.

Timeless, beside him,
sunsets will blend,
time to take flight again.

Heaven's song is void,
from every heart
when hopes, depart.

Among forever,
grace will seek,
in mournful sorrow.

The death we follow,
not for the weak,
comes tomorrow.

The Whispering Coil

The whispering coil of our hands
move us towards peace.
Slowly I dance away,
to touch the big dream.
This tether that sequesters us
to our body, falls, strangely.

Fate has its night,
flesh and bones, has its right
to explore briefly,
during this flight.
Confused by no light,
a reluctant shield crumbles

The sights cannot linger
when force jerks your fate.
It knows more than I,
It's more mortal than I.
Feeling the picture halted,
is the reason he is exalted.

Grand Design

To be overthrown,
be unknown,
is but doom. With no
eyes of a wife,
nor son,
existence has no room.
An odd story appears,
formed in darkness,
in these gutted years.

No joys or moments,
no birth , no death.
Just a shadow, formed,
to peak into this world.
A spectator of vastness,
a witness to fate,
the absence goes unnoticed,
time does not wait.

The truth forms
a heartache of stories.
Complex plots are
of grand design.
Interwoven, grateful,
the essential birth,
is that of mine.

Shallow Grave

The dead, in night,
rise to claim
the pale of your glow,
the heat of your soul.

Shadows follow the wicked
ghost, forward steps from Hell,
their hollowed heads, devoid of shame,
demons' day, their claim to fame.

The pumpkin waves
the flickering smiles.
Zombies have spoken,
the soulless have awoken.

The Disguise of a Seductive Virgin

Grapes, the cluster of nectar,
the temptation of Christs blood.
It breathes, drinks, and yields
only to itself. A weekly invitation
to a fragrant goblet.

A taste of the journey
touches boundlessly.
Anticipating a whisper
from my tongue.

Danger pleads with the disguise
of a seductive virgin.
Commune with us and bring
your tempered stare,
dance with friends.

Enlightenment

A thread, a glimpse
is all I need. Just an echo
and the dreams will yield
its due. Warriors of time
explore the new shores
of hearts, left open.

The gardens seed,
a troubadour's song
of experience, meditation.
Quiet lessons promise
enlightenment
as we go.

Swallowed

What is the point
I prayed,
the evidence shows
upon death
the world ends.
All your goods
are swallowed
and allowed
to decay.

It's a formula,
a simply one of
remembrance
and death.
Not a man
on the moon,
or does the flag
wave or not
in the wind.

Coca Cola

No more ice cream
or Coca Cola.
The TV repair man
is dead.
The Maytag guy
rests next to
the Charmin guy.
Where's the Beef?
It's in stocks
and bonds.
Laughing at
your eight dollar
cup of coffee.

Children

Maybe the children
will succeed,
only we will bleed,
so, they can lead,
us past
the greed.

Life will be fine,
as we all dine,
in what's left
of our time,
when they stop
our sudden decline.

Sunday

I wore a ripped Gumby t-shirt.
She only had four teeth.
You paint, I'll write,
It will be something
to do on a Sunday.
I'm bored, and
I'll get laid.
She can just
walk home later.

Covet

Remember me
I patched love up,
created lies
from nothing, then
spoke of the unconscious.

I showed you pain
in truth, and how
to covet disaster.
Remember me,
so, I can be.

www.ingramcontent.com/pod-product-compliance
Lightning Source LLC
Chambersburg PA
CBHW022203160726
48282CB00024B/309